LOVE, HOPE & LEADERSHIP

LOVE, HOPE & LEADERSHIP

A SPECIAL EDITION

GARY BURNISON

WILEY

Published by John Wiley & Sons, Inc., Hoboken, New Jersey.
Published simultaneously in Canada.

The images used in this book are credited to Unsplash.com, Pexels, U.S. Census Bureau, Getty Images, Adobe Systems Incorporated, and Author created.

For general information on our other products and services or for technical support, please contact our Customer Care Department within the United States at (800) 762-2974, outside the United States at (317) 572-3993 or fax (317) 572-4002.

Wiley also publishes its books in a variety of electronic formats. Some content that appears in print may not be available in electronic formats. For more information about Wiley products, visit our web site at www.wiley.com.

Library of Congress Cataloging-in-Publication Data:

ISBN: 9781394232246 (Cloth)
ISBN: 9781394291533 (ePub)
ISBN: 9781394232260 (ePDF)
ISBN: 9781394291526 (Print Replica)

Cover Design: The LAB @ Korn Ferry
Cover Image: kiwihug/Unsplash
Author Photo: The LAB @ Korn Ferry

SKY10066843_042524

INTRODUCTION

INTRODUCTION 7

SELFLESSNESS

SELFLESSNESS 21

Mission First, People Always 23
Deflect or Reflect 31
We Will 39
I'll Believe for You 47
Our State of Grace 55

POTENTIAL

POTENTIAL 63

Where Potential Meets Opportunity 65
Do We Ever Get Out of Sixth Grade? 75
Exceeding Potential 83
Second Chances 87
Our Metamorphosis 95

EMPATHY 99

Meeting Others Where They Are 101

To Walk in Their Shoes 109

Seeing Stars 115

Our Time Capsule 123

Our Five Graces 129

CONNECTION 141

Everything Will Be Okay 143

Our Connection Conundrum 151

The Stories We Tell 159

Telling Time 167

Be the Light 175

INCLUSION 179

The Journey 181

What Do You See? 185

We-dership 195

Opening the Door 205

Changing the Conversation 209

Never Walk Alone 215

AUTHENTICITY 223

The True You 225

Where There's Humor There's Hope 235

More Than the Stripes on Our Sleeve 243

LOVE 253

Leading with Heart 255

Grace and Gratitude 265

The Unopened Gift 271

On Being Thankful 275

Introduction

The concert hall was packed, and a massive grand piano stood in the spotlight.

We gave a thunderous round of applause when the pianist sat down and began to play. Then suddenly, halfway through Rachmaninoff's Third Piano Concerto, this world-famous artist stopped, rose to his feet, and announced he simply couldn't play any longer.

"We do it
because we love
the music."

It happened years ago, but I can still remember the stunned silence in that auditorium. We watched a surreal moment unfold, as the conductor left the podium, slowly approached the pianist, and whispered a few words to him.

Gathering himself, the pianist resumed playing with a passion and vigor that we had not heard all evening.

Throughout the rest of the concert, one question was on my mind: What did the conductor say that changed everything? Later, I learned of his simple but profound words: "We do it because we love the music."

For the pianist, it is the music. For the artist, it is the painting. For all of us, it is remembering why we do what we do.

After all, leading is not just about the what and the how—it's always about the who. We are all in the people business.

Reflecting on this truth, I turn my thoughts to a dear friend and one of the leaders of our firm, Bob McNabb, who fought a long fight bravely against terminal cancer and passed away several years ago. During his illness, Bob and I had hundreds of conversations. I'll never forget our last one, while I was driving my car to a university where I was giving a commencement speech.

His number popped up on the dashboard screen. It was Debi, Bob's wife, calling to say he wanted to talk with me.

Bob struggled to breathe. I could hear the hospital machines in the background. Then came Bob's usual greeting, "How are you doing, my friend?"

We only talked for a short while, but his entire focus—remarkably, but characteristically—was on me, not on him. Then he told me, "You give 'em hell," with a faint laugh.

Bob signed off as he did at the end of every conversation with almost everyone. "Love you."

And I said, "I love you, Bob." Then the phone clicked, followed by eerie silence, and I just knew. A short while later, Bob, my beloved friend, passed away.

That chair is an invitation for each of us.

That very last conversation was one of the most
emotional experiences of my life. Each time I recall
it, I'm reminded of Bob's example—he was all about
others, and with so much love.

There's an enduring lesson here. Without love for other
people, we cannot have love for what we do. Purpose
and people are always inextricably intertwined.

Think of it this way … Imagine walking into a large,
open room. All you see at the center is a long table.
Then, as the scene comes into focus, you're surprised
that seated in each chair are some of the most
important people in your life—the ones who helped
you, inspired you, changed you.

As you look from one person to the next, you also see
that there is an empty chair. That chair is an invitation
for each of us.

By following the example of those who have elevated us throughout our lives, we can aspire to be that person for whom others are genuinely grateful—the ones who offer and extend a hand. By our words and actions, we can show others that hope and humanity are not luxuries, but necessities.

So, what does that look like?

This is the question I've been reflecting on and writing about in "Special Editions" over the past four years (and counting). These aren't just my thoughts and insights—they are also backed by seven decades of world-class IP of a firm that has conducted more than 100 million assessments and develops 1.2 million people a year.

So often the focus in leadership is on what to do. But the real heart of the matter is who we are and strive to become. These elusive and often overlooked aspects of leadership are what makes these messages Special Editions.

In response, I have been humbled to receive tens of thousands of emails, phone calls, and conversations. From this outpouring, it has become clear that there are, indeed, certain key attributes of leadership.

So, if we were to ask someone to define those principles, the list would probably include such things as strategy, vision, financial acumen, growth mindset—and maybe courage, confidence, and even charisma. All true—but leadership, paradoxically and profoundly, requires more.

The real heart of the matter is who we are and strive to become.

First, last,
and always,
leadership means
other people.

What it takes to lead others is often found in the intangibles—the unseen that has just as much value as what is seen. As Albert Einstein famously wrote on his chalkboard, a favorite quote that he had taken to heart, "Not everything that counts can be counted, and not everything that can be counted counts."

That's why, in this book, our leadership attributes start with *Selflessness*—leading is never about the leader! It's helping others exceed their *Potential*—meeting them where they are with *Empathy* and *Connection* and conscious *Inclusion*. And this can only happen with *Authenticity*—and sincere expressions of appreciation and *Love*. And coincidentally, the first letters of these traits spell out the word "Special."

First, last, and always, leadership means other people. Indeed, this is the emotional, even spiritual, side of leadership. Their inspiration becomes our aspiration.

"Not everything that counts can be counted, ...

... and not
everything
that can be
counted counts."

SELFLESSNESS

This is the realization that changes everything: *It starts with you, but it's not about you.*

It's even how we define leadership: Inspiring others to believe and enabling that belief to become reality.

To be a leader means to walk with others—occasionally in front, sometimes behind, and always by their side.

Mission *first,* people *always*

It was a tale of two shoppers on my trip to the grocery store during the pandemic.

As my wife, Leslie, and I entered the store, we saw someone speaking with the manager and gesturing frantically. As we got closer, we heard the woman say, "What are you going to do about all these people getting so close to me!"

The manager tried to reason with her— pointing out sanitizing wipes for her shopping cart, explaining how the store was deep cleaned every night. None of it made any difference to her. All of it would have fallen on deaf ears because none of it answered what mattered most to her. She was frightened, and her fear was all she could understand.

Leading means meeting people where they are.

It's a reminder of the power of shared interest defeating self-interest.

Now let's go back to the grocery store. That same day, we were in the checkout line behind an elderly woman with six cans of Progresso minestrone soup in her cart—and nothing else.

"I'm sorry," the cashier said. "We have a limit. You can only get four."

Overhearing the conversation, my wife, Leslie, spoke up: "Don't worry, I'll buy the other two for her."

Immediately, the man behind us said loudly, "Count me in for four more!"

Leslie pointed to the woman's nearly empty shopping cart. "Are you sure that's all you need? We can help."

As a group of us made our way to the paper goods aisle, another shopper was just taking the last packages of toilet paper.

"Could we have one of those?" Leslie asked.

"I'm sorry," the shopper said. "I need this for my family."

"It's not for us." Leslie pointed to the elderly woman standing at the end of the aisle. "It's for her."

The shopper reached into her cart. "Of course. Take both—I have enough at home."

Stories like this are a reminder of the power of shared interest defeating self-interest.

Paint the bright lines

In the normal course of business, thousands of employees make hundreds of decisions every day. In times of crisis, decision-making amplifies—in numbers and magnitude. However, leaders in all times must "paint the bright lines"—the left and right guiderails for the actions of others throughout the organization. The leader sets the course and the destination, articulating the "commander's intent"—the mission, the purpose, the values, and guardrails. Then others must take it from there.

Let other leaders lead

Command-and-control is not the only answer in more challenging times. A directive, centralized response, yes; but at the end of the day, the decisions and actions must be made by leaders on the "front lines." Empowerment happens when leaders are willing to relinquish control. Give direction, set the boundaries, offer support, then get out of the way.

Make the message real

When leaders talk, is anyone really listening? The best way to ensure the audience is tuned in is to emotionalize and personalize communication—who we are, what we believe, what we value, and what matters most. The leader, as the steward of the organization's narrative, must ensure that authentic, relatable themes are woven into the messages they communicate.

> The best way to ensure the audience is tuned in is to emotionalize and personalize communication.

Knowledge is what we know; wisdom is acknowledging what we don't know.

It's all about the people

No leader wants to charge up the mountain, then discover halfway up that no one is following. Creating followership requires an emotional connection. What matters most is not what the leader achieves, but how people are empowered to act.

The power of believing

The leader's job is not only to show others the opening in the sky, but also enable them to punch through it. Leaders paint a picture of the future—of what's possible and how they can make that happen. If leaders wait only for others to believe in them, they will probably wait a very long time. Instead, leaders need to believe in others. When they do, they'll be amazed by the results.

Knowledge is what we know; wisdom is acknowledging what we don't know. The bridge between the known and the unknown is not the leader's intellect—it is the collective genius of others.

Deflect or *reflect*

The start of summer when I was growing up meant **endless time** playing baseball in an empty lot.

Yet I still remember that day—and the crack of the bat when one of my friends pulverized the ball with a towering shot in the air.

Then suddenly there was a reverberating crash of a window being shattered.

Some scattered, not wanting to get caught; others were just too scared to move! But when the adults asked us what happened, that's when the fingers started to point. It wasn't me ...

For most of us, these are some of our earliest life experiences—when we were totally dependent on everyone and accountable to no one. Back then, it was so easy to blame others when things went wrong—because our world was all about us.

The fact is, we all want love, approval, and acceptance. And that's why we are hardwired early on to blame others and deflect our own faults. Consequently, we spend the rest of our lives trying our best to overcome that instinct.

It's quite the paradox—knowing we're naturally one thing and fighting to be another. It's so easy to point the finger at others for disappointing outcomes while overlooking our own faults. "It's not me ... it's everybody else." Sometimes the moment clouds context.

Our firm's nearly 100 million assessments bear this out. No one is infallible. Nearly 80% of leaders have blind spots about their own skills. Our research also reveals that people who greatly overstate their abilities are 6.2 times more likely to derail than those who are self-aware.

We are all works in progress. So, instead of deflecting we need to be reflecting.

> We are hardwired early on to blame others and deflect our own faults.

Moving self-interest and selfishness to shared interest and selflessness.

Rather than trying to hide our self-interest, we need to recognize it for what it is. Then it becomes the leader's job to transform self-interest into shared interest.

When our personalities meet performance.

Our firm's research reveals five key factors for achieving superior organizational outcomes. Three are intuitive: purpose, leadership, and strategy. The other two probably don't come to mind automatically: accountability and capability. But together, they contribute about 50% of performance. The same holds true for individuals and our personalities—accountability is the all-important foundation.

First, we need to look in the mirror and see how accountable we are to ourselves.

Accountability is a good look in the mirror.

When most people think about accountability, they immediately look through the lens of how accountable others are to them. But first we need to look in the mirror and see how accountable we are to ourselves—for who we are and how we act. A person's word is only as good as the last promise kept. And, if we want to know how we're doing, we only need to count the number of times we say, "I'm sorry"—in all its forms, including "That's on me," "That was the wrong call," and "You were right."

Responsibility is in the present; accountability is forever.

It's not "what's in it for me?"—it's about shifting our focus to what we can create for others. This is the maturation process of becoming a leader ... not to deflect, but to reflect.

We *will*

Who knows how long I've loved you
You know I love you still
Will I wait a lonely lifetime
If you want me to, I will …

—The Beatles, "I Will"

It's the song our colleague Jo Schaeffer sings
to her four children every night. Except her
youngest had never been able to hear her
mother sing.

So imagine Jo's excitement when her daughter
was being fitted for hearing aids for the first
time at age six. "She asked that I be the first
voice she hears after she gets them," Jo told me.

Leadership is
not merely words,
it's actions.

To keep that promise, Jo needed to catch the last flight out of Tulsa after a client training session she was leading in Oklahoma. Then her flight got canceled. "I told people what happened. I was almost in tears. I needed to get home—it was non-negotiable," she said.

That's when someone suggested she try leaving out of Arkansas, three hours away. To make it, though, she needed to leave immediately—with some unexpected help. This was a room full of experienced leaders, including several police officers. Every participant sprang into action.

> ## It's all about transforming the desire of the several into the Will of the many.

Some people broke down the room—and others cleaned up. One police officer returned Jo's rental car to the Tulsa airport, an hour and a half away. Another officer drove her all the way to Arkansas—a six-hour round trip.

The training session ended early that day, but the real leadership lesson endured. After all, leadership is not merely words, it's actions. And that takes Will.

It's all about transforming the desire of the several into the Will of the many. So perhaps the question we should all ask ourselves is: What is our Will?

Will we be about it, not just talk about it?

It's so easy to critique, instead of construct—particularly today when differences too often overshadow commonalities. We need to be about it, and that requires looking in the mirror. The late John McKissick, America's winningest football coach, shared with us the wise words of his father: "If you don't put something in the bucket, how are you going to get anything out of it?" We need to ask ourselves: What are we willing to put in the bucket today to help ourselves and others?

Will we listen for what's really going on?

"Hey, I want to talk to you about a couple of things." When those words were expressed to me by a colleague, I had no idea at first what the conversation was going to be about. "You may be getting some feedback that I am off a bit this week," the colleague told me. "The reason is I lost a young relative." Then he tried to go to a different topic—context for a project we'd been discussing. But the more he talked, the more emotional he became. We dropped all of that and went back to the real topic—his loss. And in that moment, that's all there was to talk about. It's a reminder to all of us that the difference between hearing and listening is comprehending.

And so I asked Jo—after all that she had been through—
what it was like when her daughter received her hearing
aids. At first, there was only silence for what felt like
more than a minute as she composed herself.

"I don't know how to describe it," she said, her
voice cracking. "It was humbling … I could just see
the relief on my daughter's face … It was a look
that said, 'This is what other people experience.'"

… Your song will fill the air
Sing it loud so I can hear you
Make it easy to be near you
For the things you do endear you to me
You know I will
I will.

Indeed, that's a leadership song for all of us to sing.

I'll believe *for* you

Lost in `unfamiliar territory`, it's a stranger's guidance.

Stressed and overwhelmed, it's the colleague who reaches out. Worried and uncertain, it's a compassionate friend. And when we feel as if we cannot take one more step forward, it's the person who reaches for our hand.

We've all had those moments of doubt when someone stepped in ... and believed. One of the most memorable for me was the first time I got caught in an ocean riptide. I was young, and my initial instinct was to swim to shore, but I never got anywhere. Instead, I sank lower and lower.

Words motivate, but actions inspire.

Then suddenly, seemingly out of nowhere, an older teenager popped up beside me. "You need to swim the other way!" he yelled. "Come on, follow me!" Swimming side by side, we crossed the current and finally got to shore.

I fell to my knees on the beach, completely spent and deeply grateful. It wasn't just what the other swimmer said, it was what he did—after all, words motivate, but actions inspire.

When others are drowning in doubt, that's when we need to step up—and believe for them. Because here's the thing: believing *in* someone is an expression of confidence, but believing *for* someone is a purposeful action.

> When others are drowning in doubt, that's when we need to step up.

Whether we want to admit it or not, doubts surface all the time and for everyone, including leaders. And that's OK. When others feel discouraged or disappointed, our willingness to believe for them changes everything. Fear turns into confidence, ambivalence into motivation, despair into joy.

The fact is the leader's job is always to deliver belief. How they do that depends on leadership style, which is a function of a leader's personal characteristics, the styles used by others, and an organization's espoused values. Our firm's research, drawing on assessments of hundreds of thousands of leaders in more than 2,000 organizations around the world, has identified six overall leadership styles—directive, participative, visionary, pacesetting, affiliative, and coaching.

Our research found that the majority of leaders
only use one or two of those styles, but that the best
organizational climates are created when leaders are
proficient in multiple long-term leadership styles. In
other words, the ability to toggle—to adjust the dial.
Those leadership behaviors will then shape how others
feel, think, and engage.

Inherent in every behavior and style is belief. It must
be our opening act of leadership—and the encore that
enables belief to become reality … for others.

In life and leadership, we all have stories of people who
helped us face our fears, overcome our doubts, and
enliven our spirits. But, if we're honest, how often do
we really go back and reflect on those times and those
people who truly believed for us? More to the point, how
often do we embody those beliefs for others?

Indeed, by what we think, say, and do, we're always
telling others, "I'll believe for you—and in you."

Inherent in every behavior and style is belief. It must be our opening act of leadership—and the encore that enables belief to become reality ...

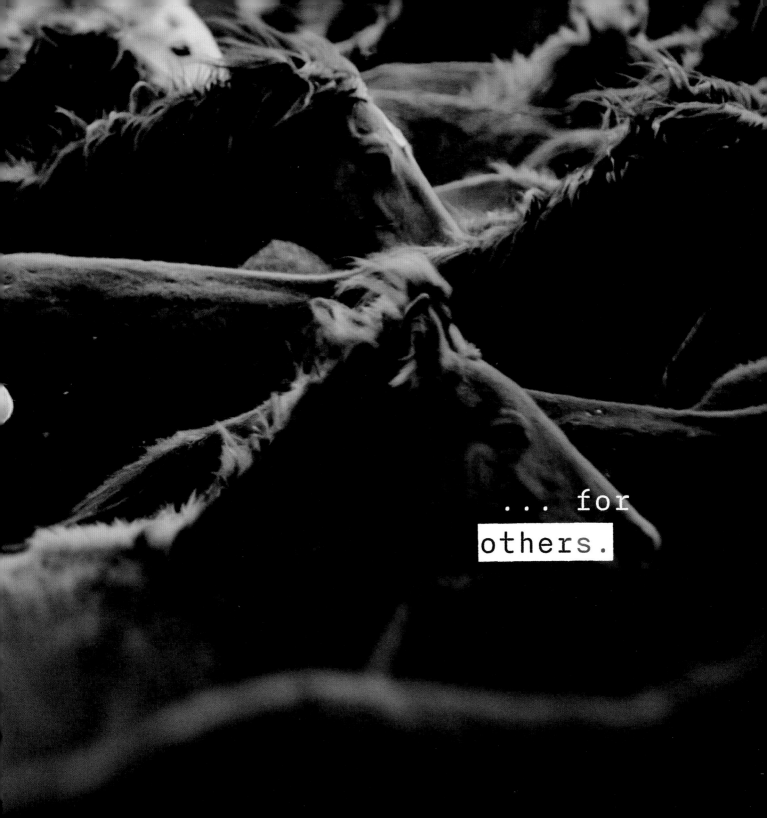

... for others.

Our state of *grace*

We didn't start the fire
It was always burning, since
the world's been turning
We didn't start the fire
No, we didn't light it,
but we tried to fight it

—Billy Joel

People turn to leaders for help and hope,
direction and decision. And that takes grace.

I've had countless conversations about grace.
In each one, it struck me that—like truth, art,
or love—grace is often hard to define. But we
know it when we see it.

Grace is a feeling.

It moves us forward—elevating above any circumstance—and always along the high road. It is what makes us inherently human—the better self that shines a light for others.

Grace is the gift of goodwill.

Unearned and unmerited, grace is present within each of us. It's as old as human history—present in all major cultures and religions. In Greek mythology, the three daughters of Zeus were known as the three Graces: Aglaea, Euphrosyne, and Thalia. Their names—translated as brightness, joyfulness, and bloom (among others)—were the gifts they gave to humanity. For us, the gift is the goodwill of a human nature that is predisposed to helping others.

Grace is an action.

The image that comes to mind may be a dancer's poise, an athlete's fluid motion. But true grace emerges through pressure and sometimes under fire. It calls us to accountability, responsibility, and action. After all, the accountability we want to see in others starts with each of us.

Grace is perspective.

When crisis strikes, our natural tendency is to think of cause and effect—to try to understand what happened rationally. But there are other forces at work—and this is where grace comes in. It is the goodness in all of us that comes out in times of pain and suffering.

Grace is the balance when emotions run high.

It is tested at the extremes when we find it so hard to be graceful—in exuberance when we need to check our ego and in pessimism when we need to overcome fear.

Grace is a virtue.

It is evident the moment someone walks into a room. They are calm and confident, to the point of elegance. It's not only their assuring words that others need to hear, but also their cadence of how and when to deliver them. And even when the answer must be "no," grace conveys positivity that makes it feel like "yes."

What truly makes a difference is the imprint we leave, and how we make others feel.

Where grit meets grace.

When the way forward is shrouded in uncertainty, grit can push us through. But grit, alone, cannot do the job—especially when leading others. Grit reports to grace—the real sovereign. No matter what happens, the only question is: Do we have the grit to be graceful?

Hope and a prayer.

I'll never forget that dinner, even though it happened 20 years ago. The occasion was a board member's retirement. As we gathered, a friend of mine walked to the head of the table and reached for a glass—his every movement radiating class. His words flowed with no script, as he quoted from memory an Irish blessing:

"May the road rise up to meet you. May the wind be always at your back. May the sun shine warm upon your face ..." Although these words were well known, we were all mesmerized, and as I looked around the table, no one moved. They weren't sure whether to bow their heads in prayer, raise a glass to toast, or stand and applaud. It can only be described as a master class in grace, not just because of the words but how they were delivered—straight from the heart.

An earthquake shakes the ground. A tornado rattles nerves. A pandemic tests resolve. In every crisis, people look to others—who panicked, who had it together. And every time, they will train their eyes on the one person who exudes confidence. This is grace—feeling, gift, action, perspective, balance, and virtue combined. Indeed, we must all ask ourselves: Are we the one they turn to?

POTENTIAL

Potential is opportunity realized—the intersection
of what was and what can be.

When we're enabling and actualizing
the potential of others, we create the next path,
the next gateway on our walk with others.

Creating opportunity should be the mindset
for leading others.

Where *potential* meets *opportunity*

The `lecture hall`
was nearly full, and
I looked out onto a
`sea of` eager faces.

Then, from the back row, a young man called out, "So, what do I need to get *your* job one day?"

The question came as I wrapped up my guest lecture at a university a few years ago. "Clearly you all have potential or else you wouldn't be here," I told the students. "But how can you *exceed* that potential?"

Potential is about **tomorrow**. Opportunity is about **today**.

Not one of them could guess the answer I had in mind.

"It takes an abundance of opportunity," I suggested,
and then the discussion went to another level.

Potential is the common denominator—we all
have potential. But it will remain a mere fraction—
substantially less than one—without the numerator
of opportunity.

The challenge, though, is that potential is about
tomorrow. Opportunity is about today.

Our progress is seldom linear. Life is full of setbacks:
the time we got cut from the team. We didn't make the
school band or get cast in the play. We didn't get the
job we wanted—or the promotion went to someone
else. In those moments, it can feel as if someone else
controls our fate.

But who's to say what someone can or cannot do?
Only with opportunity will we ever know.

It takes all of us—as leaders, as colleagues, as mentors, sponsors, and coaches, and as friends and family members—investing the time so others can achieve.

> It takes all of us—as leaders, as colleagues, as mentors, sponsors and coaches, and as friends and family members—investing the time so others can achieve.

I was barely a teenager and just learning to drive when my dad took me to the community college parking lot to practice. My dad's car was a "three on the tree"—a three-speed transmission with the shifter on the steering column. I can still remember the H pattern—first gear, second gear, third gear, reverse, with neutral in between.

I tried and tried to get it right, but that old car just sputtered and lurched, then stalled. I wanted to give up, but Dad told me to pull over. Then he put his hand over mine and led me through the gears: "Give it a little gas. Ease off the clutch." Soon, I was driving solo, and Dad was sitting back and enjoying the ride around the parking lot—a smile on his face.

That's what we all need today—for ourselves and others—with an "H pattern" that unleashes potential and puts opportunity into gear.

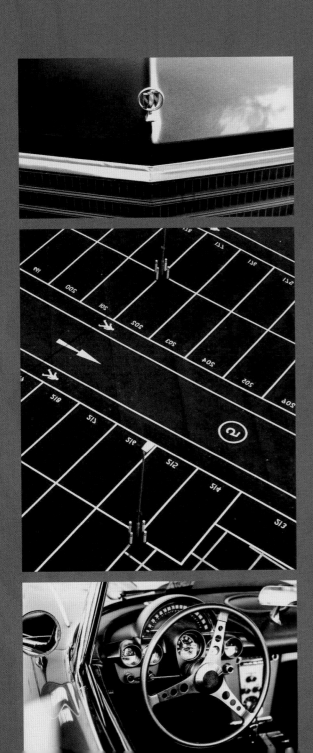

Humility.

Humility begets self-awareness, and self-awareness begets growth. Self-awareness means not only knowing ourselves, but also how and where we can surround ourselves with others who are strong where we are weak.

Hunger.

All of us have two choices. We can go with the crowd—the path of least resistance. Or we tap into our purpose—and our hunger for that purpose. Namely, our drive. That's why of all the qualities I look for in new employees, one of the big ones is hunger. Hunger manifests in many ways, starting with learning agility—the No. 1 predictor of success that's all about applying past experiences and lessons learned to new challenges and first-time opportunities. Or, as I call it, knowing what to do when you don't know what to do. Hunger also fuels mental agility—embracing complexity, making fresh connections, examining problems in new ways, and staying curious. Hunger encourages people agility—being open to diverse viewpoints and challenging preconceived notions. And finally, it empowers change agility to move beyond "this is the way we've always done things." Indeed, hunger is the bridge that takes us from potential alone into the fullness of opportunity.

Hustle.

This is the other big quality—because hustle quashes pedigree every time. It's what turns possibilities into opportunities. But here's the caveat—no one can teach us hustle. But we know it when we see it. Our research indicates that there are several signposts of potential—and all of them point to hustle. Drive and motivation. Awareness of strengths and blind spots. Hustle is the proverbial first foot on the field, last one off.

Heart

Heart.

And if there's a fourth gear—topping off our
H pattern—it's this one. Heart speaks to having the
courage to undertake the journey—and the humanness
to bring others along. For leaders, heart speaks not only
to passion and compassion, but also as importantly
to authenticity and vulnerability. The heart is where
inspiration lives and breathes.

It's true that we're all in the "why," "what," "how,"
and "when" business. But ultimately, we must be
in the business of bringing together potential and
opportunity—for others.

After all, rockets didn't take us to the moon; the
dreamers and the engineers did. The internet didn't
create a globally networked economy; it was the
innovators and creators. Since the beginning of time,
people have been the ultimate differentiator.

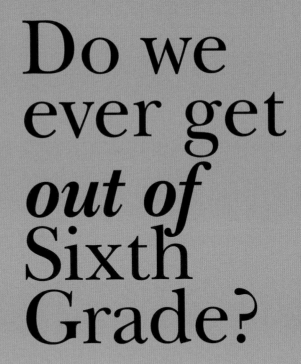

Do we ever get *out of* Sixth Grade?

The place that had once seemed so big when I was a kid was actually quite small. But it still loomed large in my memory—and for good reason.

While in the Midwest to visit relatives, I drove to the small town where I had spent much of my childhood. And there it was— or rather, where it was supposed to be. The middle school.

Our biggest
desires are
to be liked,
to be accepted,
to belong.

No doubt, these were the places where we all had so many formative experiences and lessons learned. Back then, our biggest desires were to be liked, to be accepted, to belong. Now tell me, have things really changed?

Let's face it—we never really get out of sixth grade.

As I rolled up to the school's location, I looked and looked—but where was it? Did I get the address wrong? Confused and a little perplexed, I glanced at Google Maps. Yep, this was the place.

But all I saw was a small standalone office building. The playground had been paved over for a parking lot. And that's when I knew—the hallways lined with lockers, the gymnasium, the playground. All of it—gone.

Yet the memories—and emotions—remained.

Looking back, we can remember how uplifted we felt when someone saw our potential—perhaps for the first time.

And we probably all remember how vulnerable we felt when we took the risk to try out for a team or the school play ... and our disappointment at not being picked.

I can still recall the day my dad brought home a second-hand drum set. For weeks, I practiced and practiced. When the school band held tryouts, I couldn't wait to show what I could do. The band director, though, had a different strategy: marching us around the gym to the beat of some scratchy record played over crackling loudspeakers. Afterwards, I waited as name after name was called—but I never heard mine.

> **Arguably, the workplace has replaced the schoolgrounds of yesteryear.**

So many years later, we still carry all those feelings from our metaphoric sixth grade—joy and elation, fear and insecurities. We're probably just better at handling—or hiding—these emotions.

Arguably, the workplace has replaced the schoolgrounds of yesteryear in evoking those long-ago feelings. We might even ask—just like that school, is today's workplace even there anymore? Of course, it is. It's just different.

As a firm with data from nearly 100 million assessments of professionals, we know what leads to success. There are the traits and behaviors we're born with, and the competencies we need to develop—and a shifting environment all around us. In between is learning.

Even in a different world, it still comes down to the leadership ABCs: Authenticity to take the risk to show who we really are. Believing to set the stage for achieving. Connectivity to create community.

Authenticity.

Without vulnerability, there is no authenticity. Make no mistake—it's not charisma. But people can be drawn to us if we're authentic and emotive—and we believe. It's not what we do, it's who we are that counts.

Believing.

The fact is doubts can surface at any time and for everyone. When others are discouraged, disappointed, or drowning in doubt, our willingness to believe changes everything. Fear turns into confidence, ambivalence into motivation, despair into joy. And the more people believe, the better they can achieve.

Connectivity.

To be a leader means making an emotional connection with others. And one of the best ways to do that is through stories—creating connection that leads to community. Then people become part of something bigger than themselves.

This is what we all desire. We knew it intuitively when we were back in sixth grade. And, indeed, it's what we all crave now—not only for ourselves, but for others.

Exceeding potential

"I'm going on a date," one of my daughters announced excitedly one evening during the pandemic. "We're having dinner together."

Given the lockdown, I wondered how that was going to work.

"It's by Zoom," she told me and went on to explain they were having food simultaneously delivered.

Instantly, I was reminded of the first time I heard of internet dating sites to "meet" people and wondered how that would work. Yet, it has—different times always demand another level of adaptation.

What lens are we looking through—the past, the present, or the future?

Mindset is a conscious choice—one we make every minute of every day. We need to ask ourselves: What lens are we looking through—the past, the present, or the future?

Paraphrasing slightly, we recall the words of Aldous Huxley, the philosopher and author: "Experience is not what happens to you; it is what you do with what happens to you."

"Comparison is the thief of joy." These wise words from President Theodore Roosevelt remind us of the danger of measuring today against the nostalgia of yesterday or some idealized vision of tomorrow. It's a formula for disappointment. The more we let go of the past, the more we greet the new.

> "Experience is not what happens to you; it is what you do with what happens to you."

Second chances

Slowly, she entered the headmistress's office, not sure of what to expect.

To her shock, she saw kindness on the woman's face. "I think you're being punished enough," the headmistress told her. "You don't need me to add to it."

It was many years ago, and 15-year-old Sonamara Jeffreys had been accused of breaking the school rules—"ironically, for something that I didn't do ... at least not that time," she shared with me.

There will be
times when we
need and even
ask for a
second chance.

Today, Sonamara is president of our firm's business in EMEA. But on that long-ago day, she was walking a tightrope—between her very strict mother and the headmistress of the school.

She waited outside a closed office door for an hour that felt like an eternity. Suddenly, her mother emerged. "You're staying," she said brusquely, then left without any explanation.

That's when the headmistress called Sonamara into her office. "That second chance was a turning point in my young life. After that, I just put my head down and got on my studies," Sonamara said.

When someone has been on the receiving end of compassion, they will be more likely to give it to others.

We all have flaws. There will be times when we need and even ask for a second chance. And there will be moments when we need humility and graciousness to give that second chance to others.

It's not called failure.

Think about it for a moment. When someone is given an opportunity that really tests them, there's a high probability for mistakes. It's not what counts at the moment of failure, however; it's what you do after that matters most. Instead of viewing failure as an impediment to progress, it's embraced as the pathway to actualizing potential. That's why the only real failure is failing to fail!

It's called learning.

If we're not failing, we're not learning. Sometimes, the most profound learning comes through redemption. A leader's role is to understand the past, but not stay there.

It's quite the paradox. We're hardwired for safety and self-preservation, yet we are most fulfilled when we take the risk to expose our frailties. And that's the grace of a second chance—reinventing, refreshing, renewing.

It's quite the paradox. We're hardwired for safety and self-preservation...

... yet we are **most fulfilled** when we take the risk to **expose** **our frailties.**

Our metamorphosis

Metamorphosis—it's not a choice, it's a reality.

I witnessed this a few years ago, during a time of pure powerlessness against a wave of devastation that had come out of nowhere and mushroomed into a life-threatening risk. Wildfires in California were destroying millions of acres and countless homes and costing many lives. One fire was perilously close to where I live, impacting thousands of people. Many houses in our neighborhood burned to the ground, though several (including ours) were spared by a shift in the wind.

But that was not the end of the story.

When we reflect on how far we've come, we can acknowledge and appreciate how much more capable we've become.

Heavy rains followed the wildfires. Slowly, life returned. Nature, ever resilient, greened the canyons and flowers began to bloom where, not long before, there had been only charred earth. Then one day, as I drove to the beach, millions of butterflies filled the air.

I couldn't believe what I was seeing at first—it didn't seem real. I slowed the car and watched as they sailed over the windshield, never striking it.

It was a sea of butterflies, the ultimate symbol of metamorphosis.

Sometimes a metamorphosis is apparent; other times, it's more subtle. When we reflect on how far we've come, we can acknowledge and appreciate how much more capable we've become—on the road to actualizing our potential.

EMPATHY

Empathy is the catalyst that turns words to a feeling,
then to an action.

Empathy means meeting others where they are to
understand who they are—not simply what they do. And
when that happens, they're much more likely to feel part
of something bigger than themselves.

Meeting others *where they are*

The email began with these words—
"I wanted to share my story, which I have
never shared with anyone in the corporate
world before."

The details of that story from a colleague I
will hold in strictest confidence. But I will say
that it was truly inspiring: a story of obstacles,
adversity, and perseverance—as well as triumph.
It moved me deeply.

Communication is where leadership lives and breathes.

I'm grateful that this person could be so candid and emotionally vulnerable with me to "speak about who I truly am, what my background is and, above all, for being able to view this as a source of strength."

Another young colleague wrote a heartfelt email, telling me, "For the first time, I was able to really cry and feel the emotions of all that is going on around me."

Unfortunately, sometimes CEOs and other leaders are perceived simply as a function. Their roles, however, require more. As leaders we need to show who we are as people—someone who is empathetic and can be trusted.

Communication is where leadership lives and breathes. And it must be authentic.

Challenging? Yes. Emotional? Very.

Understanding the Emotion Curve.

To be understood is to first understand others and their emotions. I think we all know the research, which shows that, during times of great change, people's reactions and behaviors follow the "Emotion Curve." On one side is the downward slope from disbelief to anger, and then hitting bottom at withdrawal. When people get to the other side, they rise through acceptance, optimism, and meaning. No one will be in the same emotional place. Leaders need to be "emotion listeners" because people don't always say what they feel. Avoidance and shock? That's denial. Going through the motions of what they've always done or avoiding big-priority conversations? That's overwhelmed. Asking questions about what the next year might look like? They're on their way up the curve.

Responding to the emotions.

Next comes the response. Leaders need to draw on their own emotional intelligence. Where there's disbelief and anger, it's all about communication—not just for information, but for connection. When people are overwhelmed, they respond to empathy. On the other side—when in acceptance or seeking meaning—people want guidance and direction. Communication is energy. Your attitude will become your team's altitude.

It's about first
meeting others
where they are
with empathy and
then transporting
them to a place
not entirely
visible today.

Communicate, always.

As leaders, if we don't communicate, we'll probably be the subject of communication—and not in a flattering way. The people whom we expect to follow—in total alignment with the purpose and strategy of the organization—will instead spend their time speculating. Why? Because a lack of communication left a vacuum that others will fill.

Even when we're uncomfortable, even when we're anxious, and even when we hit a low, we must keep communicating and leading. Indeed, it's about first meeting others where they are with empathy and then transporting them to a place not entirely visible today. A better place.

> If we don't communicate, we'll probably be the subject of communication.

To walk *in their* shoes

In the world these days, there are `so` `many` contradictions.

War versus peace. Isolation versus connection. Gray days versus blue skies. Despair versus hope. Egocentric versus empathetic. Self-interest versus shared interest.

One thing, though, bridges these gaps: the heart-to-heart connections forged in compassion. But even with that empathy, we can only strive to walk in their shoes.

Our best hope is to leave behind our myopia— the lens that often can point mostly to ourselves. Only then can we broaden our perspective and elevate our horizon to truly appreciate and understand the problems and challenges that impact the lives of others.

With greater awareness, our empathy transcends words alone to become genuine feeling—and then actions that truly uplift others.

Our journey begins
with accountability.

What we wish to see in the world begins with each of us.
In other words, we must first be accountable to ourselves
for our own behaviors. After all, when we desire peace,
we act with peace. When we value truth, we uphold it.
When we feel compassion, we show it.

We cross the bridge
to more possibility.

When we believe we can make a difference—that change
is possible—then our actions will follow.

Journey

The destination is our greater capability.

This is a broad brush: listening, caring, connecting, inspiring, expanding, exploring, and learning. Now, everything we do is grounded in the human experiences of empathy, authenticity, and connection.

This approach to leadership is not dependent on any title or position—it's for everyone. In fact, the person who will forever stand for these values is someone I knew many years ago—my friend Brett. Throughout his life, Brett was a man of modest means. But when it came to the amazing reach of his inspiring good works, he was the richest of all.

I can remember as if it were yesterday when I attended Brett's funeral. When it came time for him to be eulogized, people held back at first—waiting for someone else to go up to the podium to speak. Then came the first story— and then another.

Each recollection … helping others, caring for others … elevated into a crescendo, taking us through an entire emotional spectrum from grief to gratitude, consolation to elation. In that moment, each in our own way, we were inspired and transformed.

We may not be able to change the circumstances of people's lives. But there is that something we can do—*I see you. I hear you. You matter. I care.* Indeed, that's when we start walking in their shoes.

Seeing
stars

It was a crystal-clear night, with nothing to obscure our view. Every tiny dot of brilliance shone brightly.

My family and I went stargazing a few years ago in a remote location. Looking through a telescope, we were awestruck by the countless stars and swirls of the Milky Way. In that moment, we connected to something bigger than ourselves.

I was brought back to that experience when a colleague shared a favorite expression: *"Tell someone that there are 300 billion stars in the universe, and they will believe you. Tell them a bench has wet paint on it and they have to touch it to be sure."*

So, the question is, what are we looking for?

If we're honest with ourselves, we have probably spent a lot of time "touching the paint." In our firm's language of leadership styles, we call that directive—being deliberate and gaining immediate compliance.

The focus is usually on concerns in the moment—and in this global economic transition there's no shortage of them. Significant shifts in global trade lanes, persistent inflationary pressures, the post-pandemic reset, ongoing wars …

So how should we react?

Consider a kingdom, far, far away … Devastated by drought, the crops failed, and the ground hardened and cracked. And so, the king ordered his advisors to hire the best digging crew in all the land. They arrived with picks and shovels and began digging—six feet, eight feet, ten feet. Finally, they put down their tools. All this digging was absurd! Besides, it was hot, and they had nothing to drink.

The king was furious. He had directed them in what to do. His wisest adviser, however, suggested the king give the digging crew a tour of the kingdom—past fields that had turned to brown stubble, children sitting in the dust, cows chewing dry straw instead of green grass.

"Now imagine," the king said, "bringing life back to this kingdom."

The crew dug day and night until they struck water. When the king came to see the well, he asked the workers what had inspired them.

Their response: "We now see that what we do makes a difference."

We call that visionary leadership, which is best thought of as painting a picture of tomorrow—one that captures a larger purpose and resonates emotionally.

And being visionary and holding steadfast to belief is hard—not just in times of uncertainty, but all the time.

But make no mistake—vision is a team sport. After all, great leadership isn't simply about telling people what to do, it's inspiring them with what to think about.

When we elevate our horizon, we can, indeed, see and touch the stars.

Paint a picture of tomorrow—one that captures a larger purpose and resonates emotionally.

Great leadership isn't **simply** about telling people what **to do** ...

... it's **inspiring** them with what to **think about.**

Our time capsule

When I was young, my hometown of McPherson, Kansas, buried a time capsule filled with photographs, memorabilia, and historical records—what everyone thought people of the future should know about our community.

What if we were to make a time capsule now with tangible reminders for ourselves and future generations? What would we put in that capsule to preserve all our lessons learned?

Kindness and compassion. Empathy and connection. Resilience. If only we could distill these qualities and put them in a bottle, to preserve them—never to be forgotten. But the only way to carry them with us on the journey ahead is to keep remembering.

An executive shared with me a deeply tragic story that chilled me from the first words: "My father died in a car accident when I was 19. I was driving."

As a young driver, she swerved to miss a squirrel crossing the road, lost control, and overturned the vehicle. "It was hard not to own culpability … Forgiving myself and learning to trust myself and the world around me while learning to live without my father have been the greatest challenges of my life. I could not quantify what I would give for another minute of time with him …"

Anyone who has endured tragedies and losses would give anything to change those circumstances—but, of course, we cannot. As this executive told me, "I (eventually) chose not to succumb to the cruelty of the experience, but to live the life I like to think my father would have been proud of." Turning tragedy into triumph to honor others—this we cannot forget.

We reflect ...

Reflection is the only way to become our better
selves—as leaders, colleagues, citizens, family members,
and friends. As we reflect on who we are and, more
importantly, who we want to become, we honor the
past—while painting a vision for our future.

We reset ...

When our circuit breakers get tripped, it's time for
a reset—starting with our mindset. We leave behind
what we've done in the past and imagine how we can
do even better. But imagining, alone, does not suffice.
We put our vision into action—and our purpose into
practice. At every level, we begin to lead differently—
grounded in the human experiences of empathy,
authenticity, and connection.

We are renewed ...

Here are the fruits of the journey as our better selves
begin to take shape. We are never done. As long as we are
alive, we are always evolving.

Reflection is
the only way
to become our
better selves.

Our five graces

Like truth, art, or love—grace is often hard to define. But we know it when we see it, and when we experience it.

I'll never forget—it was early in my days as a CEO. A member of our board, who was mentoring me, looked me in the eye and said, "I don't just want you to be successful—I am going to ensure that you are successful."

I was so moved by his words, which told me that he was invested in me. Looking back now, I see it as a gift of grace.

Unearned and unmerited, grace is the goodwill of human nature predisposed to helping others.

As we all strive to become our better selves, we can find inspiration in the five graces—*gratitude, resilience, aspiration, courage,* and *empathy*. Each captures an invaluable human trait, and together they literally compose the word "grace."

Gratitude.

Even now, years later, I can still remember that phone
call ... My family and I were living in London for a few
months, and I had just flown to Ireland to visit our team
there. While I was in a cab my phone rang—and the
person calling me out of the blue was Richard Ferry, one
of the two pioneering founders of our firm. I can't even
recall exactly what he told me, but I remember vividly
the love in his voice as Richard expressed his pride for
how far our firm had come. It wasn't about him; it wasn't
about me. It was pure gratitude for all our colleagues
around the world.

Resilience.

Over the years, our parents, grandparents, and other relatives tell stories about their lives. These stories have a lasting impact, reminding us that there is always a way. I'll never forget the story shared with me by an executive about his mother who, when she was in her late 90s, contracted a serious infection that required hospitalization. As her condition worsened, the doctor gave the sad prognosis that she wasn't going to make it. The time had come for the family to arrange hospice for her. Thinking that his mother was sleeping, the executive quietly approached the hospital bed and called out gently to her. Suddenly, this woman, who had seemed near death a few minutes before, snapped her eyes open and replied, "I heard what you and the doctors were talking about. I am not going anywhere." Two weeks later, she was well enough to be discharged from hospice. Ever resilient, she lived another two years—nearly reaching 100 years of age! Moral of the story: never underestimate the indomitable human spirit. That's the resilience that propels us forward.

Aspiration.

Hope, desire, longing, yearning, wish, aim
... Each of these words speaks to an aspect of
aspiration, but it is far more than all of them.
Aspiration has nothing to do with those
momentary wants—the kind of dreams that
captured us as children. Aspiration is far more
than a passing fad or fancy. It is a vision—a
goal—capturing no less than who we are and
what we want to become. As we raise our sights,
we elevate others.

Courage.

We're in constant transition—like trapeze artists
flying through the air. We can't make the next
trapeze appear automatically—we must wait for
it. Then, as it approaches, we let go of the old
trapeze so we can reach for the new one. In that
moment—completely ungrounded—we need
courage. Courage is not about having "no fear,"
but rather to "know fear."

Empathy is not just something we talk about—it must be felt by others.

Empathy.

We see and appreciate people for who they really are. This is the power of empathy—we can literally see it at work in our brains. As our Korn Ferry Institute explains, brain imaging shows us how different aspects of empathy engage our minds and emotions. First is cognitive empathy, which allows us to understand others' emotional experiences while maintaining a healthy detachment. This is how we intellectually walk in someone else's shoes. Second is sympathy—or emotional empathy—that allows us to feel what another person is experiencing. Too much sympathy, though, can make us feel pain as if it were our own. When suffering becomes too intense, we are prone to protect ourselves by putting up barriers. Third is compassion, or empathetic care, which we experience as concern for others. This form of empathy allows us to set aside our own concerns and reach out to help. Empathy is not just something we talk about—it must be felt by others.

Grace is not defined by what we say; rather it is found in what others feel.

Life and leadership are all about the journey and the grace-filled moments along the way. Indeed, that's what truly matters—that's what people remember the most. After all, grace is not defined by what we say; rather it is found in what others feel.

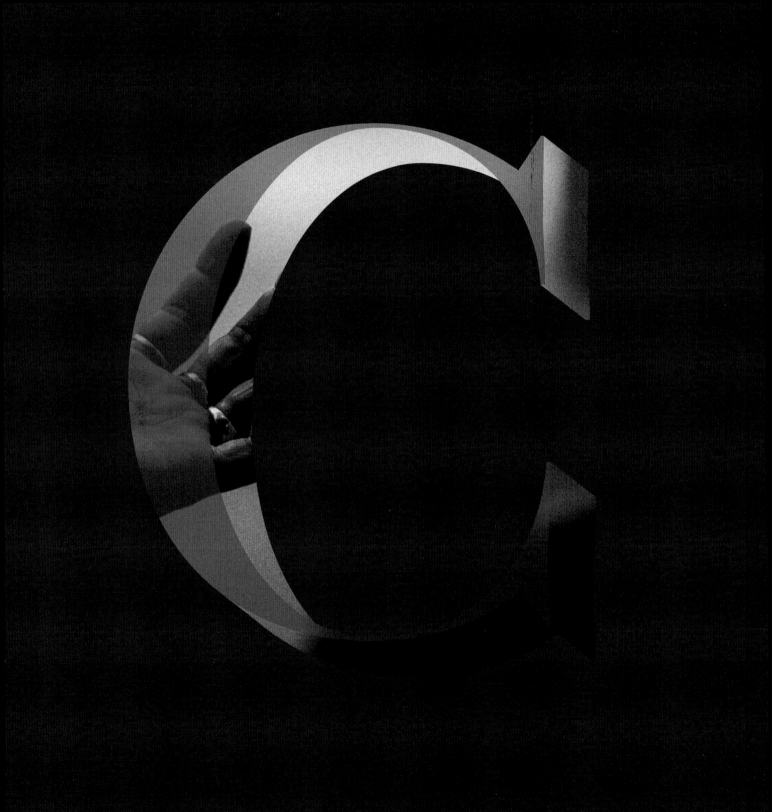

CONNECTION

Leadership requires followership. That's why to lead people is to transport them—emotionally and sometimes physically—from here to there.

To do that, we must connect with others. It's a universal need, encoded in who we are. We allow people to look into our eyes—and see our souls.

Regardless of where or how we work, we adopt a horizontal mindset—taking the time to forge connections across communities and even society.

Everything *will be* okay

As I took my dog for a walk, I came upon a stretch of pavement that literally stopped me in my tracks. Scrawled in chalk were the words "Everything will be OK."

Immediately, that child's handwriting yanked me back to years before.

My son, Jack, then five years old, was in a sterile, white pre-op room at a hospital to undergo surgery. We had all been calm the night before. But after getting up at the crack of dawn, the gravity of it hit when the nurse came in to put a needle in Jack's arm.

His eyes wide, Jack turned to me and asked, "Daddy, will everything be OK?"

Every parent, throughout time, has surely been asked this question, but for me it was the first time. Startled by the sheer fear I felt inside, I forced confidence into my voice. "Yes," I told him. "It's going to be OK."

Whether we admit it or not, this instinctual question covertly underlies conversations everywhere. Hope camouflages fear.

More than ever, the social leadership skills of the right brain (inspiring and motivating) are what give others hope.

In bull markets, people look to the leader for validation. In bear markets, they look to the leader for reassurance. Leaders are drawing on their analytical skills (their "left brain") to devise strategies—the what and the how of doing business. More than ever, though, the social leadership skills of the right brain (inspiring and motivating) are what give others hope.

Listen to educate
your intuition.

Leaders can't manage from a spreadsheet. It's all about
"walking around," tapping organizational curiosity
to get a "taste and feel" of what is happening in the
moment … what people are thinking, feeling, fearing,
and experiencing. Only with a total picture, accurately
perceiving today, can leaders accurately project tomorrow.

Connect the dots
in between.

Leadership is connecting the dots … to make a picture
emerge of what the organization will look like—and how
it will transform itself to get there. Strategy happens in
real time, nimbly adapting decision-making to changing
conditions, without losing sight of the ultimate goals.
Leaders must also connect the dots between strategy and
purpose to keep the organization on course. Otherwise,
it's wasted energy, and every decision looks like a "good
decision"—until it's not.

"The courageous have no fear."

On the wall of my home office is a beautiful, framed print—black brushstrokes against an off-white background—a gift given to me a few years ago by colleagues in China. The translation, on a brass plaque at the bottom, reads: "The Courageous have no Fear – Confucius (551 B.C.)" It is part of a longer quote: "The humane do not worry; the wise are not perplexed; the courageous have no fear." It is an expression of an ideal—an extraordinarily high bar. I view the words not only as solace but also as encouragement of what each of us can be.

By their words and actions, leaders paint a picture of what others cannot yet envision. Like the brushstrokes on canvas—or the innocence of a child's drawing on pavement—these messages give hope and instill courage. Indeed, everything will be OK.

Our connection *conundrum*

Several years ago, and half a world away.

We were complete strangers, not even able to speak the same language. But there we were—dancing in the aisles together to songs we all knew.

While in Shanghai for business, I had an opportunity to see the musical *Mamma Mia!* performed in Mandarin. Although I could not understand a single word, I did not feel like an outsider. I fit in, I belonged—bonded to others in an emotional shared experience. The music spoke to everyone, evoking a feeling that transcended language.

We need others—everyone does.

Not so long ago, neighbor to neighbor.

"We decided to do this, so that neither of us would be alone in quarantine," a colleague told me.

When everything shut down during the pandemic, this colleague and his neighbor worked out an arrangement. The colleague would work every day at his neighbor's apartment, since her space is larger and has more natural light. It worked out wonderfully for them.

Two tales—as different as can be, yet both telling the same story: of common purpose, shared interest, focusing on others, and the feeling of fitting in with unconditional acceptance.

These kinds of connections are a universal need, encoded in who we are.

Each and every day, we face the deliberate choice of kindling relationships and forging connections or else pushing ourselves deeper into retreat. After all, most of us aren't sculptors working alone, chipping away at marble in a studio. We need others—everyone does.

All of us want the same basic thing—we hear it all the time. *What's the culture like? What is it like to work there? What are the people like?*

What they're really asking—in many different ways and in different words—is simply "How will I fit it in?"

We know where this is coming from. We're all vulnerable, we all have insecurities. We want to be loved, to belong, to be part of something bigger than ourselves.

When we feel connected, we fit in. When we fit in, we belong. And when we belong, we gain a stronger sense of ourselves and who we are.

"We need uber-connectivity."

Make connectivity an action verb—showing others, by our words and actions, how to embody the pursuit of connectivity in our daily lives. It's Metcalfe's Law in action—the value of our network is a function of the number of connections. It expands exponentially with every connection we add. It happens person-to-person, from one to many, as we become part of something bigger than ourselves.

Connect, give feedback—repeat.

I remember being invited to a discussion for 150 high-potential leaders at a client. The conversation turned to connectivity—and how leaders can put it into action. The suggestion was to progress from merely giving feedback to connecting meaningfully with others. Feedback is a gift—for both the giver and the receiver. The recipient has a part to play, too. Too often when people receive positive feedback, they shrug it off as "I was just doing my job." But that depreciates the value! For feedback to forge a connection, it must be taken in.

Feedback is a gift—for both the giver and the receiver.

Top down, bottom up.

We have to be intentional in building relationships.
Learn all you can about others and then find
commonalities, especially around the deepest, most
fundamental of human needs—to be loved, to be seen
and heard, to belong.

Connectivity may, indeed, be a conundrum, but it's
also a collage—of purpose, shared interest, and fitting
in. It requires awareness on the part of the person
offering the connection—and courage for the person
willing to forge it.

The *stories* we tell

Next slide ... Next slide ... `Next` slide

Eyes glued to the screen, back to the audience, the presenter flipped through 27 carefully crafted PowerPoints. Click by click by click. But unfortunately, the audience wasn't listening.

It's a lesson I had to learn myself, many years ago. When I was a CFO, I lived and breathed the facts and figures. But when I became the CEO, people began to read my mood like tea leaves. Then, it dawned on me. What mattered wasn't just *what* I said. It was *how* I said it—my tone, energy, and attitude.

And it's true for all of us. *We are the message.*

From my first step into that office, all I saw were floor-to-ceiling shelves holding a collection of Oscars, Golden Globes, and Grammys—plus books, bobbleheads, and baseballs. Before one word of conversation was spoken, these objects told a thousand stories.

Sitting in that room was Peter Guber, founder of Mandalay Entertainment and an Academy Award–winning producer, who gave us such iconic films as *Rain Man, The Color Purple, Gorillas in the Mist,* and *Batman.*

"Storytelling is as old as human beings," he told me, his mind and words going a mile a minute. "About 40,000 years ago, if we hadn't worked together and used language, we wouldn't have survived."

The more we reveal about ourselves, the more others will share of themselves.

Of course, not everyone can give a spontaneous TED Talk or hold an audience spellbound. Nor do they have to. We just need to be our authentic selves.

To be a leader today is to be a leader of the heart. It's all about having the courage to reveal who we are.

Indeed, the more we reveal about ourselves, the more others will share of themselves.

Know our audience.

Storytelling is about delivering the exact message
that matches the time, the place, and the people. It's
not scattershot. The first step is always knowing and
understanding our audience. Who are they? What
have they been going through? What do they need and
want to hear? What experience should they be having?
What will make it relevant and meaningful for them?
Do they need to be informed or inspired, elevated or
celebrated—or all of it and more? The answers are the
difference between making and breaking a connection—
and the audience will take only a few seconds to decide
whether to tune in or tune out. But we're not just reciting
information—we're inviting participation.

The power of emotion.

I can remember being 10 years old and watching as our furniture was repossessed and carried out the front door. My dad came up beside me and, with tears in his eyes, told me, *"Son, it will be OK."* Everyone has these kinds of stories—experiences that make us stronger. And these are the stories we need to be sharing with others.

As it was for the shamans of old, who passed down lore and wisdom, so it is for us today. There is a storyteller in all of us. So, what's your story?

Telling *time*

The hands of time are `frozen` at 7:39—whether A.M. or P.M., I'll `never know`.

On my desk is a pocket watch on a chain—the one that has been passed down from my grandfather to my father to me. My grandfather carried it to work every day—first at the railroad and later at a wheat mill.

I've frequently held this watch in my hand, a tangible connection to my past. And it occurred to me—it will never tell time in the present again. Sure, I could probably get it fixed. But this heirloom is more poignant to me as a reminder to savor the past—while not trying to stay there. After all, time is the most precious of all commodities—we can't make more of it.

Time has not stood still for any of us. Nor can we simply turn the clock back and start again. That moment is gone forever.

"These things are irrelevant to fighter pilots: the runway behind them, the altitude above them, and three seconds ago."

It's like a saying shared with me by an executive who had been in the Judge Advocate General's (JAG) Corps for 33 years: "These things are irrelevant to fighter pilots: the runway behind them, the altitude above them, and three seconds ago."

This is our "telling time." We have three choices: procrastinate, pause, or push.

The starting point is to accurately perceive today—an unbiased picture of where we are, personally and organizationally. Anticipation comes next. It's future-focused, projecting beyond the horizon—Plan C for Plan B for Plan A. Navigation is the companion to anticipation—course correcting in real time.

If anticipation is the course we chart, and navigation is the ship's mast—then agility is the rudder. After all, the path of progress is never linear. But that's how we develop agility—from our experiences, both positive and negative.

Tempus fugit.

Time flies. It's wisdom as old as time itself, captured by the poet Virgil in 29 B.C.—and it's as true today as it ever was. If we become stuck in the past, we will be left behind. As Ken Blanchard, the management expert and co-author of *The One Minute Manager*, described in a conversation we had a few years ago, we all must be the "president of the present" and the "president of the future"— both at the same time.

Just like that old watch, nostalgia has its attraction—but all that remains are shadows of what was. In the words of Spanish poet Antonio Machado: "Wanderer, your footsteps are the road, and nothing more; wanderer, there is no road, the road is made by walking. By walking one makes the road, and upon glancing behind one sees the path that never will be trod again. Wanderer, there is no road—Only wakes upon the sea."

"Wanderer, your
footsteps are
the road,

and nothing more;

wanderer, there
is no road,

the road is made
by walking."

Be the light

Holiday cards were a big tradition when I was growing up. My mom would set up a couple of folding tables in the living room where she wrote and addressed more than 500 cards by hand.

In those days, everyone's mailbox was full of cards. Inside, they were everywhere! For our family, it was all about that refrigerator door where we displayed the most cherished cards. The refrigerator transformed into the light of our home during the holidays.

When our company was smaller, I tried to continue this tradition. Starting in the middle of October, I carried around a tote bag full of cards that I wrote out to hundreds of colleagues. Whenever I had a spare moment, I wrote out a few.

Unfortunately, what we all need the most—to recognize and celebrate others—is probably what we'll do the least. Yet, now more than ever, we need to create that refrigerator door for ourselves and others by sharing authentic expressions of our love and connection.

> When we connect our hearts with others, we spark hope, we kindle joy, we become the light.

Three gifts for all seasons.

The first is *connectivity*—authentic and heart-to-heart. Second, *adaptability*, which helps us look beyond what used to be—to the future that should be. Third, *receptivity*, knowing that our hearts must be open to receive, as well as to give.

Old traditions, new again.

I can remember, years ago, being at Disneyland during the holidays. It was a cold day (by California standards), and while my children enjoyed the rides, I searched on my phone for last-minute deals to someplace warmer. As I look back, to be honest, I'm embarrassed. Why wasn't it enough to celebrate in the moment?

Whatever we celebrate, however we celebrate, let us remember why we celebrate. When we connect our hearts with others, we spark hope, we kindle joy, we become the light.

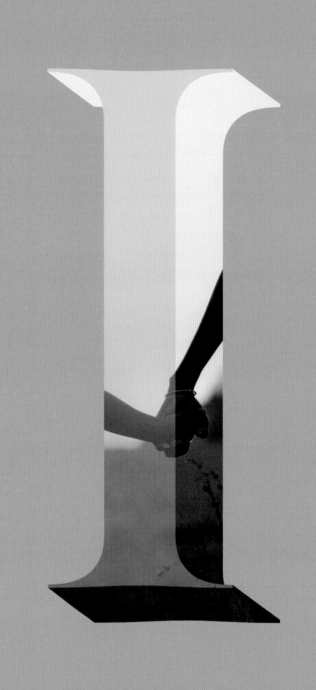

INCLUSION

Diversity is a fact.

Inclusion is behavior.

That's why we need to go beyond diversity alone to become *consciously inclusive.* As that happens, differences are not just tolerated—they're celebrated.

Consciously including others means making sure that everyone truly belongs.

The journey

Imagine you are about to embark on a journey—leading 10,000 people on a cross-country trip by foot from New York City to Santa Monica, California.

As you stand in Battery Park, at the southernmost tip of Manhattan, gathered around you are people from dozens of countries—different backgrounds, experiences, and perspectives. And your job is to lead this diverse group ...

We know that a solitary walker, putting in 10 hours a day, could cover those 2,800 miles in about 90 days. But this is not a race—it's about helping 10,000 people become more than they thought possible. Putting in about 2.5 hours a day, it will take our group a year.

A monumental challenge, to say the least. All along the way, there will be failure and success, fatigue and joy ... The unexpected will become the expected.

So, what do we need to take on this journey?

Believe ... and belief. It was one of the first calls I received on the first business day of the new year. The person on the line was frustrated with the world around us—ambiguity and constant change. "It's a new year, but the same headlines. Can we really do this again?" the person said with a sigh.

Every time I suggested—*Have you ever asked ...? Did you think about ...?*—I could never get out more than four words. The person jumped in with, "I agree, but ..."

"I get it," I said. "But the real question is, what do you believe you can change?"

The leader's job is always to deliver belief. Say it. Mean it. Act it!

So, what *shouldn't* we put in the backpack for the journey?

Ego.

It's not your amigo. When you are overly convinced you're this, you're probably that. The fine line between confidence and cockiness is humbleness. A leader will never improve a team unless they first improve themselves.

Rigidity.

Life and leadership are not linear, nor is the path to the destination. Agility rises above the rest. Plan a little, think a lot, decide always.

We are all works in progress. Some of us are striving, some are closer to arriving. It's a journey—from who we are, to who we want to be.

What do *you* see?

Has the world gotten smaller, or have our minds become narrower?

Look at the photo on the left. What do you see?

Do you notice an elderly man, walking slowly, carrying something in his right hand—a cane, perhaps? Narrow perceptions, though, can be far from reality.

We need a corrective lens.

I can remember when I was growing up in Kansas and there was a solar eclipse. Every kid heard the same warning—at school, at home: don't look at the sun!

So, when my uncle told me he could show me the eclipse, I wasn't sure what to expect. Then he took out a tall paper cup and used a small nail to punch a round hole in the bottom.

Standing outside on the street, my uncle turned the cup upside down and used the hole like an aperture in a camera to project the image of the solar eclipse on a piece of paper. I was amazed! That tiny pinhole was the gateway to the entire universe.

We all need to adjust our lens—tapping Google Earth as we zoom out before zooming in. Otherwise, we'll never imagine tomorrow's promise when tomorrow, at first, might myopically appear like today.

The world hasn't become smaller—but perhaps our perspective has. Take a look again at the picture.

The man isn't just walking down the street. He is a jazz saxophonist, making music simply for the benefit of others.

To truly see the entire picture, we must widen our lens. We need to see a world that's not about us. It's about others.

I'll never forget another walk down the street. It was about 10 years ago, and I was strolling down the cobblestones in a small town with a former world leader who led his country for several years. We were deep in conversation when the leader suddenly looked up. I followed his gaze across the street to an elderly woman with a cane, walking slowly and looking around as if she had lost her way. Immediately, he went over to her.

The woman did not seem to recognize this tall man as he listened intently, then put his arm around her shoulders and led her in the right direction. When he rejoined me, he never mentioned what had just transpired. It wasn't for show. He wasn't running for president—he wasn't running for anything. Humbly and with great empathy, he truly saw the woman and responded to her needs. Humility is the grace that constantly whispers,
"It's not about you."

We need to see a
world that's not
about us. It's
about others.

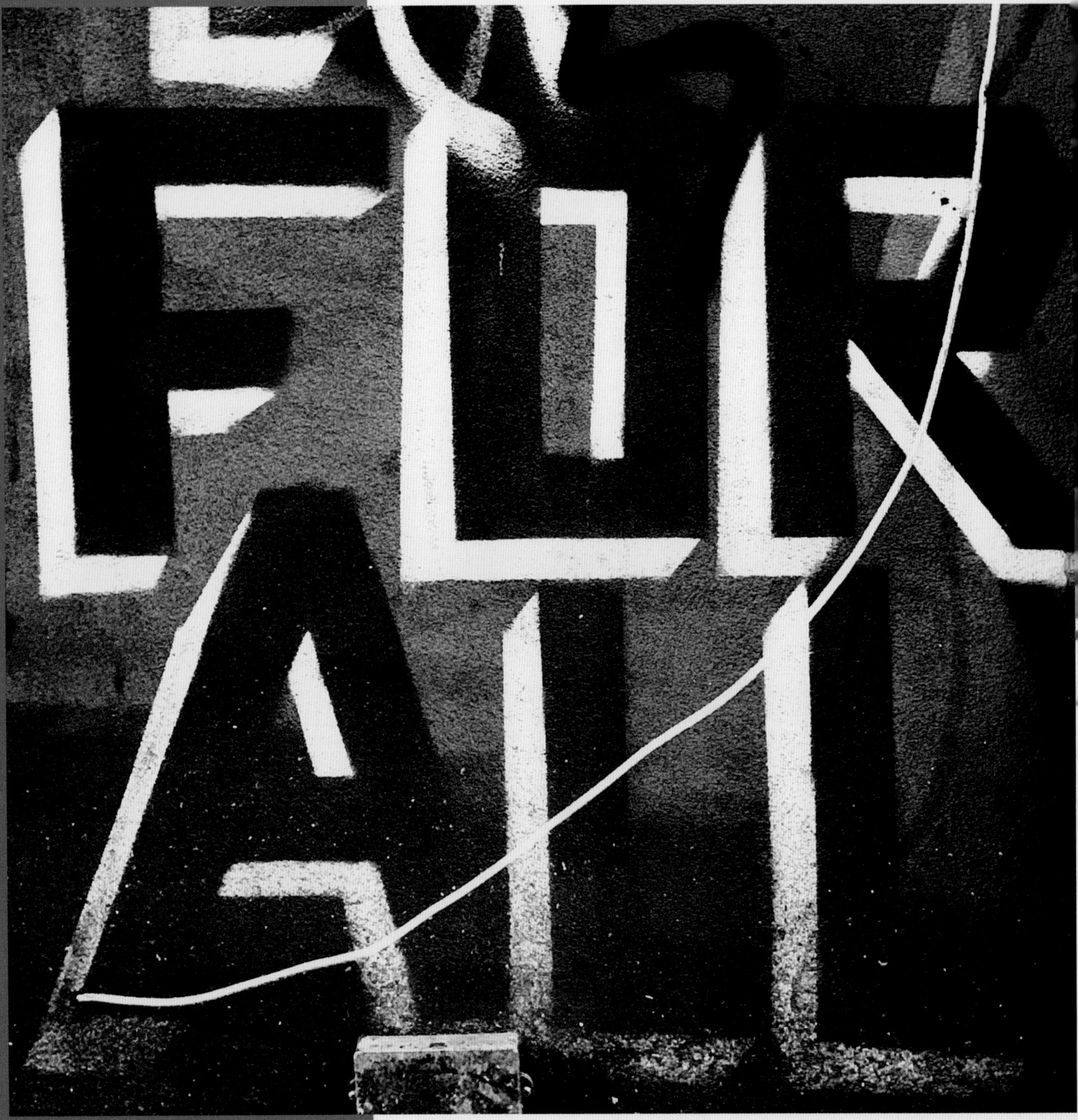

Pause, reflect, act ...

Transformation always starts in neutral, a "gear" we may not fully appreciate. It is the pause between the old and the new, between being stalled and moving full speed ahead. That pause is the "neutral zone," and without spending some time there, we can get stuck. When we go through the pause, we acknowledge that the old is dead, and the new is being built.

Open heart, open mind.

In a recent study of 24,000 leaders to identify those who are inclusive, our team noticed two basic patterns. There are inclusive leaders who "look out" as they lead with their hearts and connect through relationships. They tend to be stronger in building trust, being authentic, and being emotionally intelligent. And there are inclusive leaders who "look up" and lead with their heads as they connect with ideas. They tend to be more adaptive, inquisitive, and open-minded. Open heart or open mind—neither type is better than the other. But the key word is open.

Be conscious, curious, and serious.

To appreciate who people are takes not only understanding, but empathy *and* understanding. But here's the sobering truth: all of us have biases. Identifying our biases is fundamental to becoming consciously inclusive—where curiosity about differences is encouraged and inclusion is a mutual responsibility. Leaders need to be conscious, curious, and serious to make this happen. It starts with everyone looking in the mirror at their own biases (usually unconscious) and assumptions to ensure they do not adversely impact behaviors and decisions. The next step is for leaders to ask themselves: Are we creating an environment that demonstrates respect and appreciation for the unique characteristics and talents of each person? What are we doing— what are we saying so people can flourish? When the environment is safe, conversation will permeate.

Are we creating an environment that demonstrates respect and appreciation for the unique characteristics and talents of each person?

The more consciously inclusive we become, the more we can tap the richness of collective genius that comes from a mosaic of perspectives, backgrounds, and experiences.

We- dership

Jason stood at the top of the key, visibly trembling with nervousness.

He had to make one three-point basketball shot. If the ball went in, practice was over. If not, we kept going.

When I coached youth basketball, I chose a different player every practice to make that last "game-winning" shot. On this particular night, I chose Jason—the youngest, smallest, and the least experienced of the players. In fact, Jason hadn't made a basket all season.

He took his shot. The ball hit the back of the iron, went several feet straight up, and almost bounced in ... Instead, the whole team immediately groaned, and I heard more than a few of them say, "I just knew he'd miss it."

Then I did something I had never done before—I gave Jason a second try. "Just picture the ball going through the net," I said to him quietly. "You can do this."

Swish!

The gym erupted in cheers as the boys rushed over to Jason. That's when I turned to the doorway. I'll never forget the sight of Jason's father, his eyes damp with emotion. He thanked me, again and again—but I stopped him. "No, that was all Jason."

> **Quite simply, leadership success is measured in what others achieve.**

That was the day Jason started to believe … in himself. The real shift, though, was among the rest of the players who learned what's possible when we all believe … in each other.

Quite simply, leadership success is measured in what others achieve. Easy to intellectualize, but elusive to actualize, leadership is one part strategy, two parts judgment, three parts finesse—and four parts enabling others to achieve.

This is a playbook for every leader today— stronger together than apart.

The Me-O-Meter:

It's a simple gauge that anyone can use to assess
leadership. Listen to a leader speak. If "I," "me," and
"my" are used far more than "we," "us," and "our," then
you have to wonder about that leader's motivation.
(Even more insightful is for leaders to listen to
themselves and become aware of their Me-O-Meter.)
The only exception is when leaders are making tough
decisions and must willingly accept the consequences
of those decisions. Enlightened leaders speak from "we"
and do so almost exclusively, especially when talking
about goals and accomplishments. After all, it's the
players who win games.

Collective genius.

It's been said that the strength of a team is each
individual member—and the strength of each
individual member is the team. Given human nature,
people have their own agenda and self-interest. Add to
that personalities, pressure, stress, deadlines ... To get
beyond that, leaders need to buy into the concept of
"collective genius." What brings that group together is
shared purpose.

It's been said
that the strength
of a **team** is each
individual member—

—and the strength
of each individual
member is the team.

Putting EI into Play:

To move people and elevate teams, leaders need to use their emotional intelligence. Amid uncertainty and ambiguity, they need to "call audibles" early and often—demonstrating agility in the moment, just like the best quarterbacks do. So how do you learn emotional intelligence? Find role models—people who are good at reading others' emotions and are in control of their own emotions and reactions. Ask others for their feedback. Then set the norm for the team: this is how we interact, respect each other's views and emotions, and engage in discussions when opinions and views differ.

Today, more than ever, it's time to drop the "I"— embracing "we-dership," not self-centered "me-dership." Others always stand on the shoulders of leaders to accomplish the goals of the organization. Indeed, it's always about the team.

Opening
the door

In the town where
I grew up, doors
were **always** open.

No one thought twice about tapping on the screen door and calling out, "Hello!" as they let themselves into a neighbor's house—they knew they'd be welcome.

As leaders, it's what we all need to be doing—opening doors. It's a different take on leadership—and goes right to the heart of a question I heard in the middle of a discussion. Out of nowhere and a bit out of context, someone asked, "What's the role of a leader?" Instinctively, I went to the emotional roots of what it means to lead others: "When I think of a leader, I think of a mother, father, sister, brother."

No doubt, an unexpected response. But step back and consider what those four people represent—protector, supporter, comforter, conscience. In other words, someone willing to show others the way—not just tell them the way. And that's the essence of opening the door for someone. At the same time, the person must be willing to step inside.

Too often, though, people hesitate to raise their hands for help—and, yes, that includes leaders. Often this reluctance stems from the belief that they should already know what to do. There's a risk/reward involved, and they can't afford to appear vulnerable (or even embarrassed) in front of others. But here's the thing. No one is infallible—we all need help.

I observed someone preparing for a presentation, and as the 11th hour neared, I could sense how anxious they felt. "Look, no one knows this topic better than you," I said. "So, if you like, here's what we can do." We sat down together and started going through the presentation—shoulder to shoulder, slide for slide. I could see his confidence grow and his personality come to life. "Just like that!" I told him. The reality is, I didn't do much. He surely didn't need me for expertise—only for some assurance.

But let's face it. As leaders, we won't be able to open the door for anyone if people don't see us as approachable. My absolute favorite example of what not to do is a manager I knew several years and a few iterations ago. Wanting to protect his time for quiet, uninterrupted work, this manager made a big red stop sign and taped it on his closed office door.

No surprise—people got offended. The manager, however, was stunned. He really thought his stop sign would be helpful. Instead, the message received was "Go away." Opportunities only come through an open door. And that takes leadership.

Indeed, it's up to us to open the door.

Changing *the* conversation

It happened recently when I went to the grocery store. Stopping in the restroom to wash my hands, I looked up from the sink to see the door swing open and a young man walk in, wearing a butcher's apron with a nametag on the bib—and carrying a phone in his hand.

He headed to the far sink in the corner, propped the phone against the mirror ... and kept talking—concentrating on whoever was on the screen.

"I see you."

Glancing over, he gestured to me as if to ask, "This okay with you?"

I nodded and gave him an OK. Then he continued with what was clearly a group counseling session—given the number of voices on the phone and a professional asking specific questions around changing behavior and being honest about feelings.

As surreal as the surroundings were—a busy public restroom, with people coming and going—it also struck me as oddly refreshing. Nothing was hidden—everything in this conversation was out in the open.

When I reached for the door handle to leave, my emotions got the best of me. I gave the young man a thumbs up as if to say, "I see you."

Those words in that moment took me back a few decades, to another time and place.

Back then, I was a recent college graduate and had scraped together the money for a plane ticket to pay a surprise visit to my dad. But when I arrived, I was met with a locked door. I could hear the TV inside, but the place was dark. Only a sliver of light came from the TV screen through a crack in the blinds.

I knocked and knocked, but the door remained closed.

When I found the apartment manager and explained who I was, he let me in. I found Dad passed out on the floor—surrounded by empty bottles and complete disarray.

Not knowing what else to do, I put Dad to bed and spent the night on the sofa. In the morning, amid the stench and strewn debris, I simply said, "We've hit rock bottom—something has to change."

What came next was a courageous, tearful conversation revealing the secret Dad had struggled with for years. He admitted the truth and joined a 12-step program—I even had the privilege of going to a few sessions. Eventually, through a lot of self-reflection and help from others, there were more blue skies than gray clouds in the years that followed.

Two stories. One door flung open, one closed for too long—and both a reminder that no one can get out of a locked room by themselves.

So, when someone has an idea … *we listen*. If someone around us wants to try something new … *we encourage*. When our colleagues want to collaborate … *we welcome*. When accomplishments are achieved … *we celebrate*. And when someone deserves recognition … *we are the voice*.

And when you are the one in need … open the door.

Never walk alone

"Even after 13 years, it is a tough month."

A colleague confided to me what he has been going through, triggered by the anniversary of his grandmother's death. It's a poignant memory of the woman who had raised him—because, as he explained, "both my parents struggled with addiction and mental health issues."

But instead of hunkering down during a traumatic month, as he has for more than a decade, this time he walked a different path. By moving from isolation to inclusion, he willingly shared with friends, family, and colleagues the full array of his emotions.

This is a message for all of us—we never have to walk alone.

Every day
is a chance
for renewal.

Our conversations around well-being and mental illness are changing. Personally, I've been humbled and honored to receive an outpouring of so many heartfelt stories that have been shared with me. With incredible candor one person after another has opened up, describing *"an increasing feeling of isolation"* … being *"surrounded by addiction for most of my adult life"* … having *"fear of how they may judge me."*

Yet, rising above, they also celebrate *"opening the door and asking for help"* … *"finding the courage to share"* … *"love, compassion, and patience"* … *"unconditional caring."*

Each is a testimony to the true meaning of health and hope.

Every day is a chance for renewal. And every story shared is another opportunity to open our minds, lead with our hearts, and seek to understand.

Albert Einstein famously wrote on his chalkboard a favorite quote that he had taken to heart: "Not everything that counts can be counted, and not everything that can be counted counts."

As we look at these words through the lens of health, wellness, and awareness, it's important to recognize that just because we may not personally experience something, it is happening to others around us. It's real—and it counts. And the people and their stories are present in every workplace and environment.

This calls to mind an observation shared with me by another colleague—further punctuating the point: "What is unseen has just as much value as what is seen."

"As a leader who explicitly needs help from those around me, I am better able to see the potential of people on my team … and be a witness to their caring spirits." Those words were expressed by yet another colleague, who is dealing with a disability, as he captured his "many conflicted feelings and thoughts."

He shared with me his struggles, acceptance, and ultimately finding meaning, as he reconciles what he used to do—and what he is able to do now. Through it all, he's found a silver lining—becoming a much more connected, self-aware, and vulnerable leader.

After all, leadership is not a role—it's a calling.

"What is unseen has just as much value as what is seen."

Value

Never
walk
alone.

As human beings, not human doings, we are all easily biased toward what we see and can easily discard what we don't see. Making a connection with others, however, means observing and feeling both—the seen and the unseen.

So, how can we all travel further down this path?

Being a bit more vulnerable and a lot more authentic. Asking, listening, learning, and acting—with and on behalf of others. And always with humility and inclusivity.

That brings me full circle—to a memory of my own grandmother. I can still picture myself as a child on a cold, damp day. I was standing with one foot on either side of a floor register, trying to get warm as the furnace blew hot air into that chilled room. But the real source of light and warmth was my grandmother as she sang her favorite song.

"Walk on, with hope in your heart …
You'll Never Walk Alone."

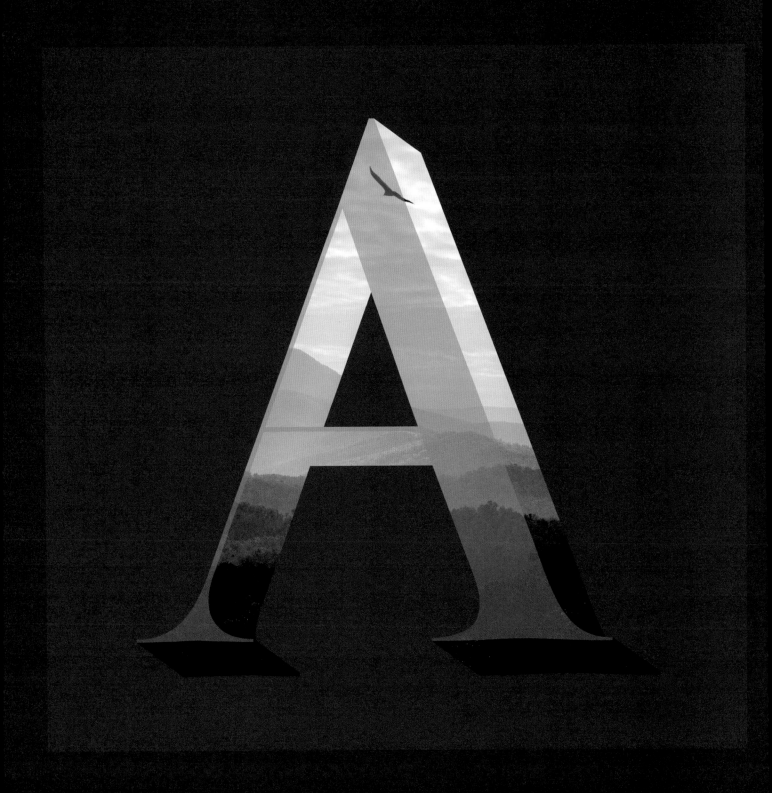

AUTHENTICITY

Authenticity triumphs over charisma—any day, in every way.

When there is trust in what we say there will be belief in what we do.

But none of us can declare, "I'm so authentic." Authenticity needs to be experienced by others.

The *true* you

Basketball practice was over. As the other kids waited outside the gym doors for their parents to pick them up, I started walking in the other direction—telling my teammates I had someplace else to be.

The truth, though, was I always asked my dad to meet me a few blocks away. I didn't want anyone at school to see my dad's old Buick, with a rusted bumper, that belched blue clouds of exhaust.

My dad had gone bankrupt a couple of years before, and we had no money. I hated going to the grocery store and always tried to pick the checkout line with the fewest people so no one would see us using food stamps.

When we tell
our stories,
others respond
with their own.

The car, though, was just as bad for a teenager trying desperately to fit in and not stand out for the wrong reasons. As I slunk low in the seat of that old Buick, my dad knew what was going on—and I knew that he knew. But we never talked about it. He just let me be.

Today, of course, I'd love to have that old Buick to restore. Even more important, I wish I could have one more chance to open that car door and sit up tall and proud beside my dad. But that was beyond what I, at age 13, could do. I was too embarrassed to know who I truly was.

Whenever I tell my story, it always amazes me how people immediately respond with their own stories. It never fails to happen. We all have our backgrounds and experiences that become the legacy we carry forward on our journey.

A great story is told about Winston Churchill when he met with a flight sergeant being honored for bravery during World War II. The sergeant had the courage to climb onto the wing of his bomber plane at 13,000 feet to extinguish a fire in the starboard engine. But meeting Churchill in person scared this officer until he was tongue-tied. Churchill noticed and said, "You must feel very humble and awkward in my presence." The flight sergeant agreed. "Then you can imagine," Churchill continued, "how humble and awkward I feel in yours."

The more authentic we become, the more relatable we are to others.

Our heads.

This is all about the technical skills that got us hired in the first place. At a certain point in our careers, though, it's assumed that we're "strategic." Not that it doesn't matter, but it's table stakes. What truly distinguishes us is our ability to connect with, motivate, and inspire others. We know from our own research that when people are heard, seen, and understood, they're more likely to be happy. And when they're happy, they'll outperform.

Our hearts.

In our words and actions, we must signal to others, "I care enough to see you." An executive recently shared with me a story from early in her career as an engineer, working in a factory. Her boss, who had worked in that plant for more than 40 years, told her, "It's gonna be real hard for you to get the respect of the floor." His advice for her was to start by learning everyone's name. She told me how she worked the line at the factory every day for an hour. "I asked stupid questions while they got a laugh from putting this young engineer to work screwing in bolts and putting pamphlets in boxes. I learned the names and stories of nearly everyone out on those lines. I was not the smartest or the most talented person working in that plant, but I had the power of true relationships." This executive took the risk of leading from her heart, knowing the reward was greater than any inadequacy she felt. Being vulnerable was her pathway to making meaningful connections.

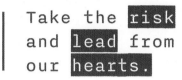

Take the **risk** and **lead** from our **hearts.**

Our guts.

It takes guts, better known as courage, to be authentic—and to act without fear of failure.

Authenticity is sometimes uncomfortable and leaves us vulnerable, and always carries with it the very human fear of not fitting in. But the greater risk is being inauthentic. Indeed, if we want to see others, we must first allow them to truly see us.

If we want to
see others, ...

... we must
first allow
them to truly
see us.

Where there's *humor,* there's *hope*

I was a new CEO, making one of my first live TV appearances.

Somewhat nervous and wanting to gather my thoughts, I grabbed an espresso-to-go and took a walk down Wall Street before heading to the studio. Mentally rehearsing my message points, I strolled through the old cemetery at the historic Trinity Church—perhaps hoping for a little inspiration from above. Instead, I got something else from on high.

A pigeon flew over and dropped a "gift"—all over my head. Stunned, I stood there in my best pinstriped suit, knowing I was going to be on air in 30 minutes.

When I got to the green room at the TV studio, the makeup artist gave me a strange look.

"You won't believe what happened," I told her and started to explain.

"You've got bigger issues than pigeon poop," she said in her heavy New York accent. "Those bags under your eyes have gotta go." Opening a drawer, she took out a tube of Preparation H, of all things, and rubbed it under my eyes to reduce the swelling.

It was all so absurd, I just started to crack up. And just like that, my nervousness was gone. Humor steadied me in the moment.

`Humor` can be a potent leadership tool when wielded with `emotional intelligence.`

We all need a time to laugh. I know that sounds completely contrarian. And it certainly doesn't mean that we should ever make light of hardships shouldered by others. But even in the depths of sorrow, laughter truly is good for the soul.

Earlier in my career, if someone had asked me to describe a great leader, I probably would have said someone with vision, confidence, courage, strategic thinking, a growth mindset. But a sense of humor—not so much. Except humor can be a potent leadership tool when wielded with emotional intelligence—*empathy*, to know what the other person is going through; *authenticity*, to see ourselves and others clearly; and *humility*, to be able to laugh at ourselves.

A few years ago, two colleagues were locked in a very tense situation. I asked them both to fly to Los Angeles so we could hash out the issues. Seeing them on the opposite sides of the conference table, I felt like we were hammering out a peace treaty. "Welcome to détente," I said, off-the-cuff. One of them smiled and the other snickered—then we all burst out laughing. It was enough to change the narrative. They weren't really adversaries; they were actually two colleagues passionately engaged in constructive conflict. By taking the personal out of it, they sparked collective genius. Instead of a battle, we got a brainstorm.

Humor, when used at the right time and in the right doses, can humanize leaders—making them far more relatable. Granted, it may not be for everyone—some people just aren't naturally funny. But when we look around and find a reason to laugh, it's like the air is suddenly different in the room. The mood is elevated, people feel energized. We see that life is bigger than whatever we're going through in the moment.

The pressure release.

At Korn Ferry, we know what great leadership looks like—and we have nearly 100 million assessments to back it up. We assess leaders constantly for traits such as emotional intelligence, self-awareness, resilience, connecting with and influencing others, and managing conflict. Admittedly, we do not assess for a sense of humor. But it does come up in some surprising ways, as a colleague in our firm's CEO and Executive Assessment practice told me. When executives are asked about how they create team resilience and optimism in tense high-pressure situations or conflict, often the answer includes humor. So, while it's not the question, it may very well be the answer. Humor is a legitimate leadership tool, and it takes a lot of intelligence (emotional and intellectual) to use it well. It can become the release valve that lightens despair and disarms conflict.

We don't build walls of words; we help people climb over to reach us.

What are you laughing at?

It's a great question for self-reflection. One of our firm's career coaches told me that she often asks people: "What is something that has made you laugh?" It always catches people off guard. After all, coaches are often speaking with people at their most vulnerable moments. A small shift and suddenly they're laughing. It's like taking a deep breath—instant perspective.

Adding a dose of levity and authenticity can alleviate even the heaviest of downpours. We become relatable. We become more human. We don't build walls of words; we help people climb over to reach us. Indeed, where there's humor, there's humanity.

> "What is something that has made you laugh?"

More than the *stripes* on our sleeve

It was an unexpected reaction—encountered for the first time many years ago when I was a newly promoted CEO. The event was a formal dinner in Latin America, and it started late, as was the custom. Three hours later ... we were still there.

Not wanting to appear rude to the hosts, I waited for others to leave first. No one did. Finally, as it approached midnight, I mentioned the late hour to a colleague sitting next to me. "No one has gotten up to leave because you haven't," the colleague explained.

Then I realized it. When people looked at me, they didn't see me as a person. They only saw the CEO—the function.

That's simply the way it is—people defer to the most senior person in the room.

We all must show that we're more than just the title, the function, the medal, the uniform, the white coat, the stethoscope ... Yes, such distinctions deserve respect. But far more important than these stripes on the sleeves are the hearts in our chests.

It starts with looking in the mirror. What do we see—hubris or humility?

It's all about our A.C.T.:

I've always found this to be true of great leaders—they're always approachable. In other words, there is no difference in how they A.C.T. It's the first and foundational principle of any interaction: being *authentic*, making a *connection*, and giving others a *taste* of who we are.

Leadership (to go):

A new CEO held his first town-hall meeting with employees. He charged up to the podium to show that he was the new boss and things were going to change. As the CEO spoke, he noticed a man in the corner who wasn't paying attention. He had on jeans, a T-shirt, and a baseball cap on backward. The nerve of this guy! The CEO called him out. "How much do you make a week?" The guy shrugged. "About four hundred bucks." The CEO reached into his pocket, pulled out a thousand dollars in cash, and told the man he should leave. The guy counted the bills with a sly grin all the way to the door. After the meeting, the CEO called one of his senior vice presidents over and said, "I sure made an example of that guy." "Yeah, he was surprised," the SVP replied. "By the way, that was the pizza delivery guy who brought us lunch. He certainly appreciated the tip you gave him." Moral of the story: lead with your function—lose credibility.

When we are truly thankful, there should be no doubt about it.

Leadership is easy to visualize, but elusive to actualize. It's not about power but empowerment … of others.

It starts with two small but extremely powerful words that translate in every language: *thank you.*

The gift we never return.

We've all had this experience: giving someone a gift and waiting for the wrapping paper to be removed and the box opened. Nervous and a little uncertain, and even to hedge our bets, we whisper when no one's listening, "There's a gift receipt at the bottom if you want to take it back." Not so with the gift of pure, unadulterated appreciation. There are no receipts, no strings attached. This is not layaway for some future obligation. It's all gratitude. When we are truly thankful, there should be no doubt about it. Others can feel it, in our words and in our actions. This gift never gets returned.

Our attitude is always our altitude.

When one person says thank you, it can set off a positive chain reaction. It's like a spark that ignites as others respond. Moods shift and positivity elevates everyone. Then our attitudes truly become our altitude.

"I am only one; but still I am one."

The power of one.

On my computer is a Post-it Note—the stickiness long worn off and now fastened with a piece of tape. On it is a quotation from Edward Everett Hale, a 19th-century social reformer and minister, that was shared with me by an executive a few years ago: *I am only one; but still I am one. I cannot do everything; but still I can do something; and because I cannot do everything, I will not refuse to do the something that I can do.* No matter how powerless we may feel, no matter how big the problems in the world, we can still do that "something" that we all can do. We can show genuine caring and gratitude.

LOVE

It's a timeless—but perhaps surprising—truth:
Leadership is grounded in love.

When we lead with our hearts, we seek to understand.
Then our words transcend into genuine feeling—and
then purposeful actions.

Our expressions of appreciation are tangible connections,
heart to heart. They endure.

Leading
with
heart

Love and leadership aren't normally put together in the same sentence (for obvious reasons). But leadership always begins with our hearts.

Face it: leaders need others—we all need others. We seek to establish a connection—with authenticity and empathy. That remains the most powerful way to change minds and win hearts.

Affirming others is more than the generic "good job" or even "I'm proud of you." Affirmation is the heartfelt "I believe in you."

When people are told, "We couldn't have done this without you," the message delivered is, "You are loved."

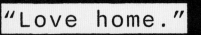
"Love home."

Sam Marks, who has worked for our firm and as a consultant for more than 40 years, often ends his conversations with "Love home." It's his unique shorthand for good wishes to the person and their family or loved ones. During a conversation with Sam, I asked him about this tagline. "It's endemic to my soul," he replied.

As he got to know more people—their lives, their families—Sam increased his use of his signature phrase by about 50 percent, he told me. "It feels more natural to say, 'Love home,' instead of just 'good-bye.'" And why wouldn't he? When we are working, we bring our families, our partners, our loved ones with us. They are more a part of what we do and our success than ever before.

We know how good it is to be the giver—of uplifting words, thoughtful support, or a small token of appreciation. Being the recipient can also be a humbling, moving experience.

A few years ago, a colleague and I were traveling through a very remote airport when we passed a boot shop. In the window was a pair of cowboy boots—valentine red. "Those are the bomb," I said, half joking. So, imagine my surprise on the plane when my colleague, brimming with a wide smile, brought out a box—yep, the cowboy boots.

The next day—as I got ready for a speech before hundreds of leaders and then a meeting with a billionaire who, at the time, was the richest person in the world—I decided to wear those boots. Not my usual business attire, but I knew my friend and colleague would be so pleased.

Even more important, though, was the smile on my colleague's face—which told me he felt appreciated for who he is.

When we walked into the billionaire's office, there were stacks of papers and books everywhere. Sitting at his desk, going over a thick report, our host was clearly distracted and did not seem to pay much attention to us as we sat down. Then, at the end of our two-hour meeting, he gave me a sly smile and said, "So, where's the horse?" We all laughed. What was truly amazing, though, was that this billionaire, who appeared unaware of anything except the papers in front of his nose, had noticed. Nothing was beyond his line of sight.

Even more important, though, was the smile on my colleague's face—which told me he felt appreciated for who he is.

The heart rules.

Vulnerability is a strength for leaders to connect with
others—authentically and with empathy. Sure, we need
to use our brains—with ideas, strategies, and analytics
that are increasingly the table stakes of leadership. And
we need courage, especially to make sure that we're
aligned with our values. But the heart matters most.

Love, undefeated.

For some, it comes down to two motivators—for love
or for money. Money can rent loyalty, but it can't buy
it. Love wins out every time. People want to be loved
and they want to belong—and the most potent rewards
address both of those desires. That can be done through
a sincere congratulatory email, recognition on the next
Zoom conference, or even a simple "thank you." We can
never say "I believe in you" too often.

I see you. I value you. You matter. You make a difference.
These powerful, affirming words mean one thing:
You are loved. At a time when we need to lead with
heart, what more is there to say?

Grace *and* gratitude

When I was a kid, holidays meant going to the Elks Lodge in our town for a special dinner.

It was a big deal. My uncle, who worked in an oil refinery, and my aunt, who was a nurse at the town hospital, would take us. We wore our "Sunday best"—my uncle with his dark green one-piece jumpsuit (which, for some reason, had a belt) and his white leather dress shoes. I'd sit there with my aunt and uncle, surrounded by neighbors, in a room decked out with twinkling lights.

What I wouldn't give to be back there, just one more time. I'd pay anything for that experience— just to be with them again, knowing what I know now. It's all about the moment and the meaning.

Indeed, relationships should be our real abundance.

"Did anyone tell you how great you are today?"

It's what we all need to have—and who we strive to be for each other. And that's our saving grace. Leadership is having the aspiration—to be an inspiration for others.

Have we told everyone how great they are?

Gratitude is timeless and has no expiration date. I'll never forget the story an executive shared with me a few years ago—about her 92-year-old grandfather who made it a habit to deliver a heartfelt message to everyone who made a difference in his life. Whether he was speaking to family members and friends, or someone who served him at the local diner, he always said, *"Did anyone tell you how great you are today?"* Reflecting on her grandfather's words, which she'd heard thousands of times, the executive told me, "It still snaps me out of whatever mindset I am in and humbles me into a simpler state of mind—of being loved and seen." Indeed, gratitude makes all the difference.

Our helping hands.

I was sitting on a curb along a highway in Oklahoma. I was driving a rental car along an unfamiliar road. Cell phone reception was sketchy, so with a conference call coming up, I pulled to the shoulder and found a place where the signal was strong. That's when another vehicle pulled up. "Do you need help?" the driver and passenger asked me. With sincere thanks, I assured them I was fine. The whole interaction took only a few minutes, but I will never forget it. And this is what we constantly need to offer others—wherever, however, and anywhere we can.

A foundational truth.

From place to place, season to season—the landscape will always change. But a foundational truth remains the same: It starts with us—but it's not about us. Offering love and support to others means keeping everyone motivated and aligned—the optimist and the pessimist, the curious and the cautious, the introvert and the extrovert, and everything in between—as they leave the familiar for the unknown.

Love is about supporting everyone—the optimist and the pessimist, the curious and the cautious, the introvert and the extrovert ...

The *unopened* gift

I'll never forget the story Bob Rozek, our CFO, told me about when he was ten years old—and loved hockey. And all he wanted for Christmas was a pair of real hockey gloves. On Christmas morning he opened the biggest box first and was surprised to read "men's galoshes" on the cover. He set that box aside and didn't think any more about it as he opened a couple more presents.

Several months later, knowing his season was over, his aunt called to ask him: "Hey, how did those gloves work out?" At first, he had no idea what she was talking about. Then it dawned on him, and he started digging in the back of a closet where he found the galoshes box. As he started to open it, he teared up. There were those brand-new gloves—exactly what he'd wanted all along but never able to realize their potential.

Sound familiar? When we only focus on what's missing, sometimes we can't see what's right in front of us.

> **It starts with reflecting on who we are and who we want to be.**

A recipe for gratitude.

There is much that we all can do. It starts with reflecting on who we are and who we want to be.

- Do I spend the time making sure someone feels better after an interaction with me versus how they felt before?
- Is there daylight between my words and my actions?
- How do I provide meaning to others?
- Do I just assume people know I appreciate them, or do I actually take the time to tell them?

May we each have the grace to be grateful— for others.

On being
thankful

It happened at a gas station in Minnesota, a dozen years ago ...

Doug Klares, one of our firm's leaders, was waiting for an egg salad sandwich at a convenience store when he picked up a slightly crumpled newsletter lying on the counter. Humble looking, with holiday clip-art graphics, that newsletter from the operations leader at the gas station chain was hardly something you'd expect to make a lasting impact on someone's life.

Then Doug started reading.

Name the six wealthiest people in the world ... Name seven people who were honored as Time Magazine's Person of the Year ... Name the winners of the Super Bowl for the past five years ... Name four of the biggest-selling box-office movies in the last twelve years ...

Doug couldn't come up with more than a name or two—and that was precisely the point. The same thing happened to me when he shared the newsletter, just the other day.

Then came the epiphany from that newsletter.

Name a teacher who made an impact on your life ... Name one friend who has always been there for you ... Think of someone who inspired you to be better ...

A lot easier to answer, isn't it?

"Who is on your list?"

These are the people who truly influence our lives—who, by their words and actions, genuinely make a difference. Simply because they care.

So I asked, "Who is on your list?"

Doug didn't hesitate to answer. "My dad," he replied, his voice choked with emotion. "I lost him on 9/11."

No wonder he has kept that gas station newsletter all these years. In that extraordinary wisdom, from the most ordinary of places, he finds comfort and a constant reminder of the person who had the greatest impact on his life.

Our memories of those who have made a difference in
our lives help define who we are, how far we've come, and
just how capable we've become. For some, that message
is a pick-me-up in a challenging time in their career. For
others, guidance on how to lead by meeting people where
they are. And for all, it offers a thankful perspective.

So who are we grateful for? And do we strive to
be all that they have been for us—as a leader,
a colleague, a friend?

Because here's the thing . . .

First, last, and always—leadership is about inspiring others to believe and enabling that belief to become reality.